D1426674

the LITTLE BOOK OF BAR BETS

A LEGALLY RESPONSIBLE WORD

Now... let us make something quite clear, this is not a book about gambling. That would be illegal and both the author and all concerned at Headline would never do something like that. Never. They are all far too nice and responsible (well... except for Emma my editor, she's downright filthy and is barred from all reasonable drinking establishments in London). This is a book designed to teach you a few party tricks that will leave your friends in no question as to how utterly utterly brilliant you are.

And yes, you may wish to challenge your friends to a drink. That's not gambling, that's just being a tight-fisted smart-arse and there's nothing illegal about that.

But if you do scrounge drinks using these tricks then we're far too responsible not to point out that you shouldn't drink more than government guidelines. Bad things happen when you drink too much. And I don't just mean ending the evening chucking up in the gutter and shouting 'I'm cleverer than that Derren Brown, me!', or going home with someone that – come the clear and painful light of morning – is so terribly unattractive you feel the need to take a scouring pad to your eyes before donating the rest of you to medical science.

the LITTLE BOOK OF BAR BETS

AS SEEN ON THE REAL HUSTLE

GUY ADAMS

<u>headline</u>

contents

36

84

70

START BETTING!

cash in Hand

The Bet

Ask your lovely – and hopefully wealthy – drinking companions to fish in their bulging wallets for a note. Tell them to fold that note in half, then half again. This will be their stake. Their choice will be a simple one: they will either give you the money or ask you to double it. Surely, they think, that is no choice at all.

Now ask them to clasp their hands together, fingers interlaced **(1)**. It's almost as if they're praying not to lose their money. Not that it'll help.

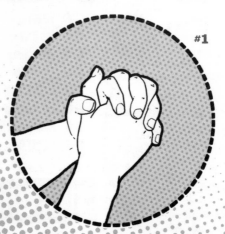

#1

Once they've done that, tell them to extend the third finger on each hand. (Help them if you wish; it's in your best interests, after all.) Slip the folded note between the tips of their extended third fingers and then make your proposition clear **(2)**: if they wish you to double their money, then they should drop the note to the table; if they hold on to it, then you'll assume they're happy for you to keep it.

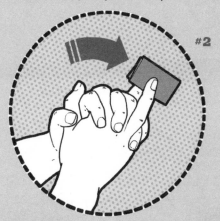

#2

The Solution

With their hands clasped in such a manner, it's impossible to separate the extended fingers.

There's nothing more you need to do, other than finish your drink, watch them squirm, and then help yourself to the offered note.

ALTERNATING SHOT GLASSES

#1

The Bet

Set up a row of six shot glasses on the table. The first three are full; the rest are empty **(1)**. By moving only one glass, can anyone arrange them so that they alternate between full and empty? If anyone can, then – because you're nothing but fair – you'll buy them a drink. (And no, bashing the other glasses out of the way isn't allowed; they're full of precious, easily spilled alcohol, for God's sake.)

Sit back and watch as your friends try to make their brains work. Hopefully, they'll keep moving the same glass, looking more and more dense as they realize they have no idea what to do with it. Give them time, repeating the helpful phrase: 'You can only move one glass.' (This is helpful – to you – as the word 'move' keeps them trained on picking up a glass and placing it somewhere else.) Once you feel everyone's been tortured enough, it's time to quench your thirst. Offer to show how it's done, requesting a drink for your efforts – one from each person, of course. Genius is thirsty work.

The Solution

Pick up the full shot glass in the middle, empty its contents into the middle empty glass then return it **(2)**. The glasses are now in perfect alternate order.

#2

Height VERSUS Circumference

The Bet

This is a simple one. All you need is a standard British pint glass (you know the sort, bulbous at the top, none of your straight-sided or fluted nonsense). Ask which is greater, the height of the glass or the circumference of the rim?

Chances are, your table will go for the height of the glass, but let's make sure, shall we? Start the bet off at a beer – nothing too major – then up the ante. Grab a couple of packs of cigarettes (or whatever comes to hand if you're inside or sat at a healthy table), stack them up and then put the pint glass on top. Again, ask which is the greater, the height of the pint glass and the packs combined, or the circumference of the rim? It must be the height, mustn't it? A beer and a shot says it isn't... Grab something else, a mobile phone perhaps, and build the stack higher.

By now, your mates are desperate to win their bet, so of course they'll increase the stake to a couple of beers and a shot. Now add something else... your wallet, if it's flat enough (and given that you rarely pay for your own drinks, you clever person, it's unlikely you've come out loaded). Surely the combined height of the stack must now be greater than the circumference of the rim? Everyone at the table will be desperate to prove it – after all, you can tell just by looking at it, can't you?

No, of course you can't... They should know better than to bet with you.

The Solution

Time to put them out of their misery and get on with drinking your profits. A standard pint glass is 15cm tall, with a rim circumference of a whopping 27cm. You can afford to build quite a stack and still be on the safe side of this bet. You can measure by wrapping a serviette around the rim then dangling it next to the stack.

Who said geometry was boring?

27CM

The Bet

Pick one of your friends and ask them to nominate the person in the group with the weakest vocabulary (not including you, of course, they wouldn't dare...). When they have selected someone, ask the selector how many words the selectee can list in two minutes without the letter 'a' in them. Feel free to help them along by giving a few suggestions: 'soon', 'being', 'conned'... words like that... How many could they come up with? Ten, perhaps? Twenty?

Your suggestion of ten or twenty will help to keep their claim realistically low. However many they suggest – and this will depend entirely on how many drinks you've already had: there comes a point in most successful evenings where even a short sentence is a challenge – bet them that the person they nominated as having the lowest vocabulary can list at least fifty... no, you feel brave, ninety... without the letters a, b or c. In fact, they can list ninety words without the letters a, b, c, j, k or m in them.

You'll give them two or three to get them started, just as you did when explaining to the mark originally, but thereafter they're on their own. If they do manage to

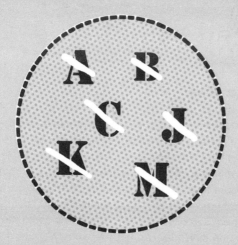

list ninety words in two minutes – and for a person of apparently such poor vocabulary, it'll be a miracle if they know that many, surely? – then the original mark buys everyone a drink. If they don't manage, then you'll get the round.

The Solution

As promised, you give the mark's choice a few words to get them started: 'One, two, three...', and then tell them to keep going. When counting from one to ninety-nine, none of the words contain the letters a, b, c, j, k, m (or, indeed p, q or z). So as long as the selectee is capable of counting, your bet is as good as won.

BRidGe BUiLding

The Bet

Place three wine glasses in a triangle in front of you. They should be fairly close to one another but with enough space between them so that the rims of any two adjacent glasses do not allow the third glass to be balanced on top of them. (Or not without the following trickery, at least.) Remember to drop a couple of matches next to the glasses **(1)**.

The proposition is this: the third glass must be balanced on top of the other two – without moving those two, naturally; that would be too easy – using only what's on the table (but excluding whatever receptacle their drinks happen to come in). You are so confident that nobody will be able to figure it out, you say, you will happily bet a round of drinks on it. Put your money where your mouth is and place a crisp note on the table in front of you.

#1

14

#2

The Solution

Your friends naturally mess about, trying to use the pair of matches to balance the third wine glass on the other two. This is, of course, impossible and therefore good fun to watch!

Once they have given up, take the note on the table and fold it lengthwise into a tight concertina so that it's strong enough to act as a bridge between the two glasses, then place the third glass on top of the note (2). It should go without saying that a little practice wouldn't go amiss – nobody's going to be impressed if you dump the glass on top and it falls off! It's perfectly easy but, like most things in life, make sure you're good at it before doing it in company.

shot Down

The Bet

We all like a shot now and then. They're ideal for those points in the evening when a larger drink represents too much effort for not enough return.

For this bet, pick one of your friends and wager that they won't be able to drink a shot you place down in front of them. Make a few things clear to start off with. You will not cover the shot glass. It will be right there on the table and perfectly easy to pick up. There'll be nothing nasty in the shot glass (nothing they would gag on trying to drink). It'll be just a normal shot – whatever they fancy, in fact. All they have to do is to drink the shot in five seconds without spilling a single drop. If they do, then you will buy the next round of drinks; if they don't, the round is theirs.

> "All they have to do is to drink the shot in five seconds without spilling a single drop"

The Solution

To make this work, you need a playing card, or similar (anything thin and laminated). You place the card on top of the shot glass, turn it over face-down on the table and slip the card back out. The shot glass is perfectly accessible; it can be picked up at any time. But if they know a way of doing so – in only five seconds – without spilling a drop of it, then they're a genius and deserve a free drink.

on a Knife Edge

The Bet

You need four wine glasses and three knives for this one. Arrange three of the glasses in a triangle. Leave the fourth glass and the knives to one side.

The challenge is this: the fourth glass must balance on a structure made from the other three glasses and the three knives. All three glasses and knives must be used. Each glass must support only one knife, each knife must touch only one glass and the fourth glass must be resting on the knives rather than the other glasses for support. Easy, eh?

The Solution

Take two of the knives and hold them parallel, their blades pointing towards one another and overlapping in length. Then take the third knife and weave it between the other two blades (so, with the knives facing you, it passes behind the first and in front of the second) **(1)**.

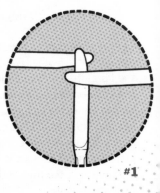

#1

18

#2

Then, keeping the central knife where it is, bring the handles of the other two up forming a Y shape. Let the tip of the left-hand knife cross over the blade of the knife on the right **(2)**. Now the blades of all three knives are woven over each other, forming a triangle in the centre (and if you can read this without needing a drink you're a stronger person than I... just look at the picture to make sure you've got it right while I pour myself something strong... meths over ice perhaps).

A Trial in Separation

The Bet

Take a pair of empty pint glasses, the British sort (at the rate you keep winning drinks, it shouldn't take you long to get a collection going), and stack them one inside the other. The challenge is to place them in any position you wish (standing on their base, upside down, on their side, wherever...) then to separate the glasses without touching them. Allow your friends to try it, sip your drink. Hmm, almost empty, that will never do. Time to win a refill...

The Solution

Once your friends are utterly stumped (and hopefully before they've managed to smash the glasses in sheer frustration), offer to show them how it's done, all for the price of just one more drink. When you position the glasses, place them, carefully, on their side on the very edge of the table. The inner glass should be free of the table's edge entirely. Now, blow sharply between the two glasses. The air pressure will push the inner glass out of the first, and you can catch it just in time for it to be filled with the alcoholic beverage of your choice.

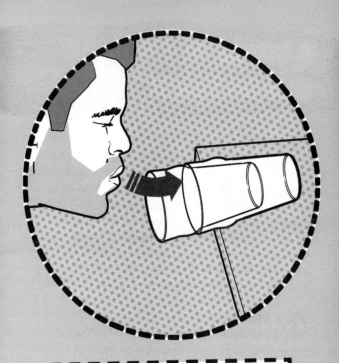

"Allow your friends to
try it, sip your drink.
Hmm, almost empty,
that will never do.
Time to win a refill"

A CAREFUL SNIFTER

The Bet

In order to perform this you have to buy your own drink for once. Not to worry, you can always ask for a refund to be part of the price of you revealing the secret!

Pour a measure of brandy into a large, balloon brandy glass. What the mark must do is to drink that brandy. Naturally, there's a catch. Place a tall, slender sherry glass upside down inside the brandy glass. The brandy can only be drunk from the sherry glass, and you can touch the brandy glass with your hands but not the sherry glass **(1)**.

The Solution

This is not a bet to be proposed late in your evening of unpaid-for boozing, as it requires a little practice. Lean over the glasses and, with the top of your head pointing towards the table, grab the far edge of the sherry glass base between your teeth (therefore not touching it with your hands) **(2)**.

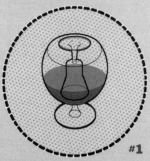

#1

22

#2

#3

Lift the sherry glass out and, by clenching your teeth, allow it to flip upright so that the bowl of the glass is resting against your nose.

> "Practise, get it right, then try it out"

You can now pick up the brandy glass and pour the brandy into the sherry glass. Turn the brandy glass upside down and slide the base of the sherry glass on to the base of the upturned brandy glass. Put the lip of the sherry glass to your mouth, and lift it from below by holding the brandy glass. Phew! Now you can drain the brandy (3).

See, told you it was one to do after practice and while sober. Nobody's going to buy you a drink after you've whacked yourself in the face with a sherry glass and poured brandy in your eye. Practise, get it right, then try it out.

the lifting match

The Bet

A little preparation is needed for this one. Lay a matchbox flat on the table with a match inserted into a hole so that it stands upright at one end, with the ignitable tip facing upwards, when the box is laid flat. Now place a coin flat on the box and balance another match on top of it at an angle so that its ignitable tip leans over to touch the tip of the upright match.

I need a drink just trying to describe it but, put another way, the matches form two sides of a triangle with the box as its base. The challenge is to remove the coin without knocking over the matches.

The Solution

Using another match, light the touching tips of the matches. As they burn, the tips mould together and the leaning match curls upwards, lifting free of the coin. You can now pull the coin out gently, having not touched the matches at all.

"The challenge is
to remove the coin
without knocking
over the matches"

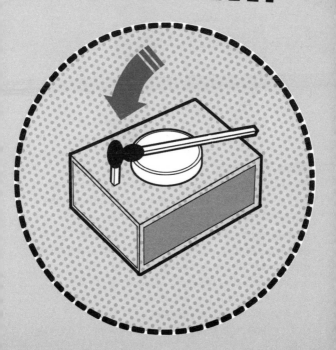

the FLYing Egg

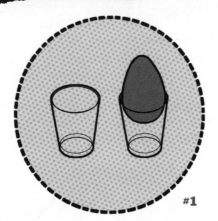

#1

The Bet

For this proposition, you need a pair of shot glasses and an egg. Yeah, I know, you always take an egg out with you when you go drinking, don't you? Perhaps once you've learned this, you'll start (or only perform this trick when drinking in a bar that serves food; chances are, a kitchen will lend you one).

Place the shot glasses 4 or 5cm apart, one directly in front of you and one behind it, then drop the egg into the glass closest to you.

The challenge is to move the egg from one glass

to the other. Easy enough until you consider the rules: you cannot touch the egg and, while you can touch the glasses, you cannot alter their position or lift them totally clear of the table.

The Solution

Tilt the glasses towards one another then blow sharply on the egg. This will cause an air current to move over the egg's surface, knocking it forward into the empty glass. Practise a little at home to get the positioning of the glasses right and the strength and positioning of the blow needed to tip the egg.

#2

COIN GAME

The Bet

A charming little game this, like noughts and crosses – or Tic-Tac-Toe, as our American friends call it, for reasons best known to themselves – but with a whopping great round of drinks to be won at the end of it.

A square serviette is placed on the table next to a pile of coins (the coins must be identical, all the same size and not too small; you don't want to be playing this for hours). Each player takes it in turns to place a coin on the serviette, the loser being the first player unable to place a coin so it is completely on the serviette (no part of the coin must hang over the edge).

Tell your opponent that it doesn't matter who goes first; they're free to choose. Once that has been decided, the game begins, and it's only a matter of time before your thirst is quenched.

The Solution

If your opponent chooses to go first, explain that the game always starts with a coin being placed in the dead centre of the serviette, and put one there. If they wish you to go first, simply place that central coin as your first move. From there on in, the key to success is simply to mirror your opponent's placement of their coins. If they place a coin on the far corner to their left, then do the same. If they place a coin directly to the right of the coin in the centre, you do the same... If you play the game this way, it's impossible for you to lose: there will always be a counter-move available to you up until the bitter end. Symmetry – a gift to drinkers the world over!

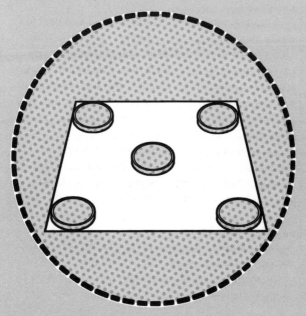

spin the bottle

The Bet

Another proposition that requires practice (and perhaps a dustpan and brush, and a nurse on standby as your opponent throws beer bottles all over the place).

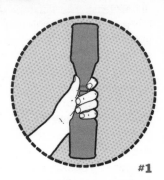

The challenge is exceptionally simple. Start by holding two empty beer bottles in one hand, one on top of the other, their mouths pressed together (**1**). Now try to reverse them so that their bases are touching. You can only use one hand and you cannot put the bottles down or rest them on anything.

The Solution

To achieve this, you need to master a series of moves:

Step one: Allow the upper bottle to drop so that you're now holding both bottles by their necks, their bases towards the floor.

Step two: Throw the forward bottle upwards and catch it as close to the base as possible. Then shift it so that you are gripping its base with only your index finger and thumb.

Step three: Relax your other fingers slightly so that you are now gripping the second bottle loosely by its neck, its mouth pressing against the base of the first bottle **(2)**.

Step four: Twist the lower bottle so that it's

#3

at right angles to the upper one, its mouth pointing outwards, away from the other bottle **(3)**. Turn your hand so that the lower bottle is now on top (and the other bottle upside down), then walk it down your palm with your fingers until both bases are together.

Then learn to play the piano. You're obviously dextrous enough.

31

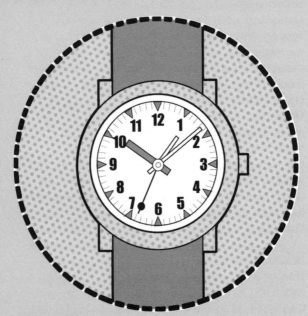

The Bet

Wager that you can ask your friend three simple questions about their watch. If they get one of them wrong, they buy you a drink; if they get all of them right, you buy them a drink. The questions will be simple and not concerned with the inner workings of the watch. Agreed? Good... then tell them to cover the watch with their hand so they can't take sneaky peeks. Then ask the questions:

Question one: Does it have a hand showing the seconds? Now, some do, some don't and, hopefully, your watch-owner has paid enough attention over the years to know the answer. Tell them to uncover it quickly, just so we can all check whether they are correct. Bang. Cover it up again.

Question two: Does it have the Arabic number six on it? Many don't, they may have a roman numeral or even no number at all, just a mark at the correct spot on the watch face. Once the watch-owner has given the answer, as before, the watch should be quickly uncovered to see whether they are right or not.

Question three: What's the time?

The Solution

How often have you checked the time on your watch only to forget it immediately? Odds are, they won't be able to answer you, or certainly not precisely. It goes without saying that 'about ten past eight' does not win a drink! What you've done here is distract the watch-owner away from the whole point of a wristwatch by focusing their attention on trivial details.

change for a shot

The Bet

Placing a full shot glass on the table, rest a pair of coins at opposite sides of the rim. The challenge is to be able to drink the shot without either touching the glass or letting the coins fall to the table (**1**).

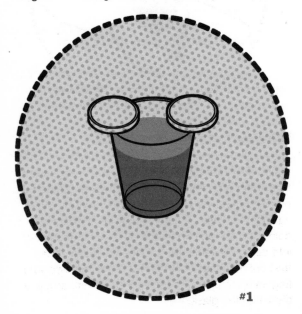

#1

#2

The Solution

The key to this is learning one move: with your
thumb and forefinger, brush the outside edges of the
coins, knocking them to either side of the glass then
pinching them instantly so you are squeezing them
against the glass **(2)**. As you are only touching the
coins, you are able to lift the glass without coming
into direct contact with it. Once you have done
this, put the glass back on the table and slide your
fingers up to bring the coins over the rim, dropping
them into the glass.

Hats off to you

The Bet

Here's a nice one that's guaranteed to have your mates grinding their teeth as they buy you your drink. As long as they're not grinding your teeth with their fists, who cares?

Place a full shot glass on the table and cover it with a hat (or a serviette perhaps – anything that hides the drink from view). Announce that you can drink that shot without touching the hat. Holding up a straw, explain that, while you will use the straw to drink the shot, you won't use it to touch the hat. Impossible, no? Certainly that's what your mates will think.

Bend down, point the straw towards the brim of the hat and suck. Then lean back and declare the job done and ask for your drink.

The Solution

Of course, your mates won't be satisfied with that. They'll demand proof. They lift the hat – and, eventually they must, as you refuse to do it. As soon as they do, pick up the drink and drain it with your straw. Challenge achieved. You didn't have to touch the hat at all. They did it for you.

"Here's a nice one that's guaranteed to have your mates grinding their teeth as they buy you your drink"

tied up in knots

The Bet

For this, you need someone wearing a tie, so it's ideal if you're in the pub when the office monkeys clock off for the day. Not like they don't deserve it after all, 'Hey Steve, you got that spreadsheet showing the sales spike indices for the third quarter?' No mate... but I have a got a thirst on and a con that will have your hair-gel encrusted head hopelessly baffled (and your credit card screaming... have you seen the prices of drinks in these city bars? Anyone would think it was liquid platinum you were quaffing). First, tell them to remove the tie (no need to encourage any potentially fatal accidents). The challenge is this: they must hold each end of the tie in either hand and, without letting go at any point, make a knot in the middle of it.

Having presented the challenge, sit back for a few minutes and watch as your chosen victim writhes around looking as if they're doing the hand jive, before putting them out of their misery.

The Solution

All you need to is pick the tie up correctly. Fold
your arms first, then grab each end of the tie.
Now all you have to do is pull your arms apart
and you'll automatically be left with a knotted tie.
And a baffled city boy. And a nice new drink.
The first of many perhaps...

the impossible
hole

The Bet

This one needs a banknote, two coins (one larger than the other), a pencil and a pair of scissors. Yeah, I know, you don't normally head out for a drink carrying craft tools, but when there's free booze to be had, you'll carry anything.

Place the small coin on the note, draw around it, then cut a hole the same size in the note (if you're squeamish about this, then you can just use a piece of paper – but the bank will let you off if you ask nicely, promise).

Challenge anyone to push the larger coin through the small hole in the note. They cannot tear the paper; the hole must be left utterly intact.

The Solution

There are two ways around this, one cheeky solution and one that relies simply on science. The cheeky solution is to place the larger coin on the table, poke the pencil through the hole and push the coin along the table with it (you have, after all, just pushed the larger coin through the hole). The more impressive solution – and the one less likely to get you beaten up – involves folding the paper. Fold the note twice along the diameter of the hole, once lengthwise, once widthwise, therefore folding the paper into quarters. Now, keeping the note folded in half, put your fingers either side of the fold and push. This widens the hole, allowing the coin to pass right through.

BOTTLING It

The Bet

Place a banknote on the table. This may seem like a brave move on your part but don't worry too much, with your track record you'll have owned the note for many years, never having had to spend it. You certainly won't be losing it now either. Place an upturned beer bottle on top of it, the remains no doubt of your last free drink **(1)**. The challenge is to remove the note from under the bottle without either touching the bottle or letting it fall over. Yes, another one for the clean-up crew and Band-Aids, it's a daredevil existence being a hustler.

#1

The Solution

As with a few of these bets, this definitely needs practice. Only ever present these challenges when you're confident of being able to pull them off yourself. Mastering this takes a steady hand. (Maybe use another proposition to scam

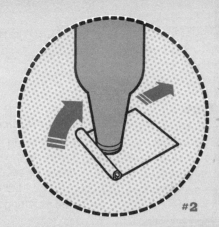

yourself a brandy first, just to settle your nerves.)

Roll the note into a cylinder, moving it slowly towards the bottle (2). When the rolled note reaches the neck of the bottle it will begin to push it along the table. As the weight of the bottle is pressing down and the pressure forcing the bottle along the table surface is delicate and right at the very base, physics keeps the bottle upright. If you move too fast – if the pressure you are applying at the neck becomes greater than the pressure applied downwards by the weight of the bottle in other words – the bottle will fall over and you'll look silly. Take it slow and gentle, eventually the bottle will be clear of the note so you can pick it up and put it back in your wallet where it belongs.

the REVERSE POUR

The Bet

Another challenge that relies on our best friend: physics. Take a wine glass that's only a third or so full and pour what remains into a saucer. Now, insist that you can get most of the liquid back into the glass without touching the saucer.

The Solution

This is one of those perfect little propositions that looks so impossible your friends won't even know where to begin. To achieve it you need a book of matches. Open the matchbook and stand it in the shallow pool of liquid, the tips of the matches facing up. Light the matches and, after allowing them to burn for a moment, lower the wine glass, inverted, over them. The flame will go out and the glass will fill with smoke. It will also start to fill with the liquid as the vacuum inside the glass sucks it up. Physics – we'd never get free drinks without you.

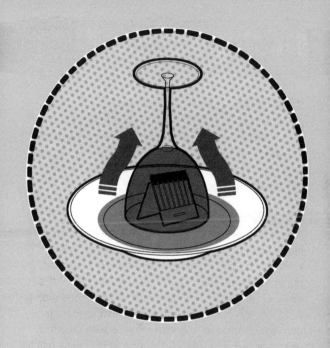

"This is one of those perfect little propositions that looks so impossible your friends won't even know where to begin"

The Bet

We all like to impress, and a bit of flattery usually goes a long way. Pick your target and comment that they look strong – maybe they even lift weights from time to time? Even if the only thing they lift on a regular basis is a beer glass, they will probably respond favourably. While that warm glow is still bubbling, ask them which arm they favour: are they strongest with the right or the left? If they say the right, tell them you know something you could put in their left hand which they would be able to lift easily, but not if they tried using their right. So, to be clear: you know something they could lift easily with their weaker arm but not lift at all with their stronger. Would they like to prove their strength by accepting your challenge?

The Solution

Place the elbow of their strongest arm in the palm of their weakest. They'll be able to lift that easily enough, but it would take a very strange physical defect to be able to lift that elbow with the hand at the end of it.

COIN BALANCE

#1

The Bet

This is another proposition that requires a steady hand. Place your driving licence on the rim of a glass so that one end juts out over the edge like a diving board **(1)**. Then ask your friends how many coins they think they could stack on this end before the licence topples off. The coin must be placed beyond the rim of the glass, so that it's full weight is bearing on the licence and not being supported by the glass itself. Not many, they'll say. Well, for sure, you reply, but however many they can stack, you will be able to stack more. A round of drinks says so (and that never lies).

The Solution

Your friends try to drop coins on the end. Chances are, they don't even manage one. The trick – because of course there is one – is to fill the glass right to the brim with liquid **(2)**. The surface tension of the liquid clings to the underside of the driving licence and will allow you to stack a number of coins on the end of the licence.

#2

A POOL SHARK HUSTLE

The Bet

A lot of pubs and bars have pool tables, and it would be a shame not to take advantage of one to win a few drinks. Place a pool ball inside the triangle in the centre of the table and offer the challenge. Can anyone pot the ball inside the triangle (using the cue ball and a cue, naturally) without removing the triangle?

> "A lot of pubs and bars have pool tables, and it would be a shame not to take advantage of one to win a few drinks"

The Solution

Placing one point of the triangle directly towards a side pocket, simply hit the cue ball against the dead centre of the triangle's base. The triangle pushes forward, knocking the ball inside forward as it does so. The point of the triangle travels over the hole before stopping against the cushion. The hole is now inside the triangle and the ball falls into it.

shaken not stirred

The Bet

For this, you'll need a martini glass and a pair of dice (so, ideal if you happen to be drinking at the *Casino Royale* – try not to get shot). Hold the martini glass in the crook of your index finger and thumb, and pinch the dice, one on top of the other, between the tips of those fingers. The challenge is to get both dice inside the glass using only the hand you're holding them with.

The Solution

The top dice is easy enough*: flick your hand up so the dice is thrown into the air, then catch it in the glass. The second is a little more tricky. Throw it up gently but then make sure to lower the glass to catch it rather than raising it, so you don't lose the dice you've already caught. Practise a few times to get the moves perfect and then reward yourself by getting someone else to fill the martini glass for you.

*Okay, so strictly speaking 'dice' in the singular is 'die' but through the fact that most people didn't know that and just said 'dice' anyway the latter has become the standard singular term in

modern English. Part of pulling these stunts off
is confidence so if anyone pulls you up on your
grammar, tell them what I've just told you, then poke
them in the eye for being smug. Never let a sucker
get the upper hand, these people need to remember
they are nothing more than walking vending
machines for your not inconsiderable thirst.

FLOATING MATCHSTICK

The Bet

Lay one pint glass on the table (the European or American, tall and slender glasses work best), hemming it in place by standing a pair of glasses either side of the narrow, lower section. Take a match from a full box and use it to make a bridge between the sides of the upright glasses (you may need to snap it in order for it to fit: it's important that the beer glass lying down remains trapped between the other two; also, make sure you do not break off the sulphur tip). The challenge is to remove the glass that's lying down without letting the match fall.

"The challenge is to remove the glass that's lying down without letting the match fall"

The Solution

Taking another match, light the sulphur tip of the wedged match. Just before the match has burnt completely, gently blow it out. The burnt sulphur tip will adhere to the surface of the glass. If you remove the other glass, the match will stay in place, fulfilling your only stipulation in this challenge, and you can pick up the horizontal glass easily.

POP the CORK

The Bet

Push a cork all the way into an empty wine bottle so that it ends up rolling loose inside (where that lovely wine used to be, sloshing about and being all brilliant). The challenge is to get the cork back out without breaking the bottle. Perhaps an unopened bottle of wine should be the stake, that seems a fair price don't you think? And when you finish that one there's no point in letting an empty bottle go to waste, why not challenge someone to see if they can get the cork out of it? If they can't then you could show them how it's done, as long as they agree to buy a new full bottle of course, and when you've finished that then there's no point in letting an empty bottle go to waste, why not challenge someone to see if they can get the cork out of it? If they can't...

Hmm... I think we can all see where this is going, it's likely to be a long old night...

The Solution

To pull the cork out, you need a length of thin material that you can poke into the neck of the bottle. A silk or light cotton scarf would be excellent, but any thin cloth will do. Once there's a reasonable amount of the

material inside the bottle, roll the cork on to
it and slowly pull the material back out. The material
becomes trapped between the cork and the neck
of the bottle so that, as you pull, it drags the cork
free. See? Easy! You could do it in your sleep, which,
after all the bottles of wine you're about to drink, is
just as well.

A cash Float

The Bet

If you've had a successful night with your proposition bets thus far, then chances are the bar staff will be only too happy to help you out on this one. After all, you've sent a fair amount of business their way. Don't be surprised if you end up on commission. (Unless you've been using these challenges on the bar staff, of course, in which case, expect to be barred before the night is out.)

Suspend a banknote inside a pair of European – or American-style pint glasses, the glasses

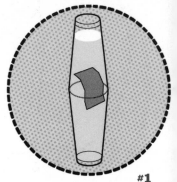

#1

inverted so they are rim to rim. The glasses are filled with water, leaving you with cash floating in the middle of what is, in effect, a glass tube of water **(1)**.

The challenge is to remove the note without spilling all the water (a few drops are acceptable, but only a

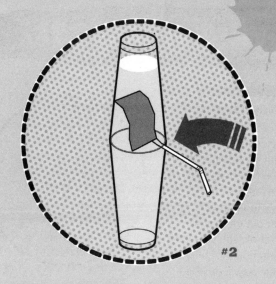

#2

few – otherwise, the bar staff will stop being your friend pretty damn quick).

The Solution

Chew the end of a straw to flatten it, then carefully insert it between the two glasses. The surface tension of the water will allow you enough movement to get the thin straw in place without drenching the table (2). Then hook the banknote and pull a corner out from between the rims of the glasses. Once a piece of the note is out, you can then slide the whole thing free.

LOST IN A GOOD BOOK

The Bet

Time for someone with your next drink in their wallet to fish it out and put it where it belongs, a man could die of dehydration around here... How about a little trial of strength? There's nothing a beer-swilling lad likes more than the chance to prove he's harder than Chuck Norris dipped in concrete.

We've all heard about people who can tear phone books in half, but this proposition seems far more reasonable (not least because it doesn't involve lugging a phonebook around with you). Offer two paperback books, one on top of the other, to your would-be Hercules. All they will have to do, you explain, is take one in each hand and pull them apart. You promise you won't stick them together with glue or tie them up... it will just be the books. Seem easy? Of course it does... when will they ever learn? It's never easy unless you know how.

The Solution

Interweave the pages of one book with the pages of the other so that they are meshed together. Squaring the books up, offer them across the table and, however hard your victim tries to pull

them apart, they won't be able to. The friction of the paper creates too strong a bond. Before they do themselves a mischief suggest they take on a physical task they're more capable of: carrying a drink from the bar all the way to your table.

A Cheeky Vintage

The Bet

Who doesn't like a glass of champagne every now and then? We all need a bit of class in our lives, after all. Here's a way of getting a bottle for the price of a single glass. That's the sort of bargain offer we hustlers specialize in.

Take a glass of champagne and tell your friends that you have a little challenge for them (if you have any friends left, that is – you're getting to be expensive company). Get the bar to bring you a sealed bottle of champagne. Explain that you can drink from that bottle without breaking the seal, removing the wire or damaging the cork in any way. If you can't, then you will happily pay for the bottle. If you can do as you say, however, then the bill's all theirs.

The Solution

Invert the bottle and pour some champagne from your glass into the deep recess on the bottle's base, then cheerfully drink from it. You have lived up to your promise, and can safely chug away at the rest at no cost to yourself.

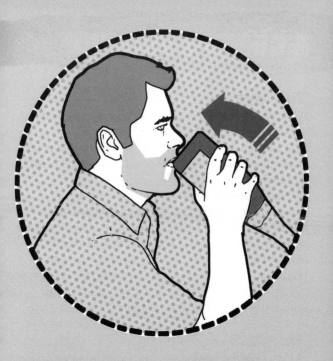

An Extra Note on Phrasing

If you ensure that your glass of champagne is exactly the same vintage as the bottle that forms the prize in this proposition, you can even promise to 'drink that champagne from the bottle...' as, grammatically, you would still be perfectly correct. An ideal way of misleading your friends even further.

the impossible shot

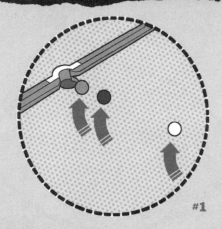

#1

The Bet

A nice sporting challenge for use in bars with a pool table. Place a red ball near the mouth of a centre pocket with a black ball (or a ball of any other colour) directly in front of it but about 5cm away. Then place the cue ball – again, in a direct line – 30cm or so back from the black **(1)**. The challenge is this: can the red be potted without the black being touched? The player is not allowed to use any of the cushions.

The Solution

No, you cannot use the cushions, but nobody said you couldn't use the triangle. Place the triangle over the black ball, its point nearly touching the red. Now all you have to do is gently hit the triangle dead centre on its base and the point will knock the red in, leaving the black ball untouched (**2**).

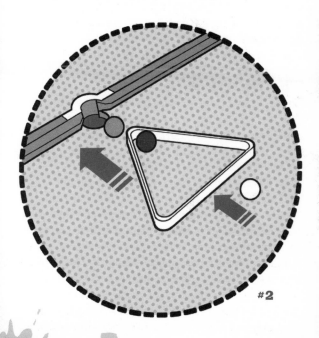

#2

WATER INTO WHISKY

The Bet

Fill one shot glass, with whisky and another with water. The challenge is to put the whisky into the water glass and the water into the whisky glass, effectively having the drinks swap places. You can't use an extra glass, your mouth or a straw. Just the sort of hustling genius you are, by now, famed for.

The Solution

No, you cannot use an extra glass, but you can use your driving licence (or any other flat, waterproof card). Placing the card over the mouth of the water glass, tip it upside down and place it directly over the whisky glass. Now move the card slightly to allow a small gap between the glasses where the liquids are touching one another. Water is heavier than whisky and it will naturally force itself downwards into the whisky glass. The only way it has room to do this is by forcing the whisky upwards. After a short period of time, the two liquids will have completely swapped places.

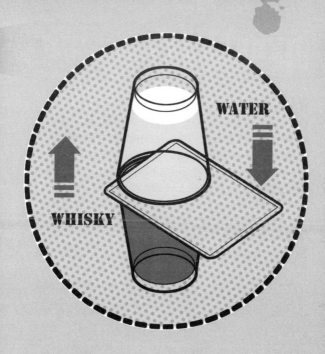

WATER

WHISKY

"Just the sort of hustling genius you are, by now, famed for"

matchbox balance

The Bet

What would the thirsty hustler do without a box of matches? Never has so useful a device been built with which to con your fellow drinkers out of a round. Some people think they're just for lighting cigarettes, you know...

This proposition seems utterly painless. Upturning a large glass in the centre of the table, lay an empty matchbox flat on the base of the glass, with enough of the box poking over the edge that you can get your fingertip under it (1). The object of the exercise is to flip the matchbox up to stand on its end. You can only use one finger. Simple, eh? In fact, why not prove it as such? Let them do it once, just so they can see how easy it is. Now, with everyone convinced, it's time to play for drinks. Somehow, the trick can't be repeated – the box topples over just as it

#1

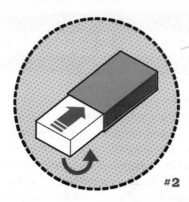

#2

seems on the verge of standing upright. Have you put something in the box? Open it to prove you haven't, then settle down to drink your drinks.

The Solution

All you need in the matchbox for this trick to work is the cardboard drawer that holds the matches. When you play the game first, ensure it is sitting normally, the solid base facing down. Then,

when it comes to playing for drinks, turn it over so the drawer is upside down, the solid base facing upwards. Sell this move by separating the drawer from the box to show your victims it is completely empty then put it back in reverse **(2)**. Now, that slight extra weight of the underside of the drawer facing upwards is just enough to topple the box forward whenever someone tries to flip it.

SPiN the GLASS

The Bet

Bet that you can take a flat-bottomed glass and, holding it only in one hand, spin it around twice. You can't let go of the glass – trying to spin it on the tips of your fingers is likely to have you spraying your gin and tonic everywhere – and it will be gripped in your hand the whole time **(1)**.

#1

#2

The Solution

Place the glass flat on your palm and grip it with
your fingers. Now, holding your arm straight down
against you, turn your wrist anti-clockwise, and
swivel your elbow to revolve the glass one full turn.
Now lift your arm from the shoulder, initially to a
45-degree angle, then lift your forearm, bringing it
over your head and back round **(2)**. The glass has
passed through two full revolutions.

the Backspin challenge

The Bet

What you're proposing seems a simple test of strength – but then nothing is quite what it seems when you're the one making the bet, now is it? Standing at the end of the pool table, place a pool ball on the upper edge of the table. The challenge is to press down on the ball so that it shoots on to the table, but who can make it roll the farthest? Your victim takes first go and probably manages to make the ball roll 30cm or so. Now you take your turn and send the ball rolling right up the table, winning the challenge easily.

"Licking the ball would also work, but you'll look an absolute tit, so don't"

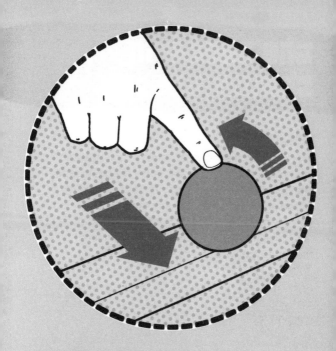

The Solution

When you press down on the ball the friction between your finger and the ball causes backspin, which, however hard you squeeze down, will soon stop the ball's momentum. However, if you lick your finger first, the friction is minimized, allowing the ball to travel much further. Licking the ball would also work, but you'll look an absolute tit, so don't.

the PaPeR BOTTLe-OPeNER

The Bet

Bet that your mark cannot remove the metal cap from a beer bottle using only a sheet of A4 paper – not his teeth, for God's sake: beer's nice, but it isn't worth shattered molars and bleeding gums.

#1

#2

The Solution

Fold the paper lengthwise down the middle, then again, then again, then one final time. Four folds in all **(1)**. Take that long strip and fold it in half, then again. By now you have a solid length of paper, which – if you flatten the folded end slightly to give you a leading edge – will be a strong enough lever to prise the top off the bottle. Use your hand at the neck of the bottle to flex the lever against **(2)**.

75

caught in a BOTTLENECK

The Bet

For this, you need an empty beer bottle and the metal cap that was on it. The cap should be bent in half – a test of strength before you even begin. Now you are ready to offer your challenge. Explain what must be done. The folded cap must be placed inside the bottle; drop it into the bottle to illustrate your point. The bottle can be placed on the table however the victim wishes and they must then remove the cap without actually touching the bottle. Then tip the cap back out, and offer both it and the bottle to whichever brave fool you wish to buy you a drink.

The Solution

You don't actually say that the cap must be dropped into the bottle. You said it should be 'placed' (and the fact that you dropped it in while talking is neither here nor there; they should know you're a tricksy sod by now, so it's their own damn fault). Place the cap just inside the neck of the bottle, then carefully lay the bottle on the edge of the table. Blow sharply into the neck of the bottle. This will dislodge the cap.

"The cap should be bent in half — a test of strength before you even begin"

BALLOON LIFT

The Bet

You have two glass tumblers – avoid any with heavily weighted bases; they will only make your life more difficult and possibly see you fail, something that no hustler worth their salt could bear – and a party balloon. Obviously. Who doesn't go out without one? Mug a clown if you can't find one of your own.

The challenge is to lift the two glasses using only the balloon. You are not allowed to touch the glasses at all while lifting them (which will scupper any sly git who tries to wrap the balloon around both glasses and lift them that way).

> "Who doesn't go out without a party balloon? Mug a clown if you can't find one of your own"

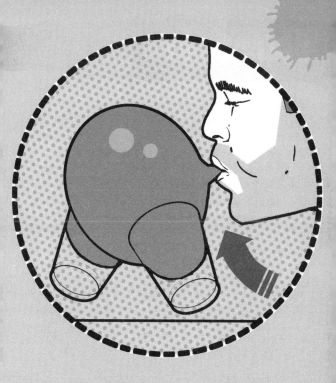

The Solution

Tilt the glasses so they're touching mouth to mouth then drop the bladder of the balloon between them and blow it up. The balloon will force itself into both glasses allowing you to lift them.

thumb lift

The Bet

Placing an empty beer bottle on its side on the table, explain your challenge. Can the bottle be lifted using just your thumbs? There are some rules: you can only hold the bottle right by the mouth of its neck, it must stay horizontal while being lifted and you cannot put your thumb inside the bottle.

Tricky? Not when you're you, and in the mood for a free pint.

The Solution

Place the bottle on the edge of the table then interlock your hands with your thumbs facing the neck of the bottle. Rather than grip the bottle with the tips of your thumbs, as everyone else no doubt tried to do, squeeze it between the joints above the knuckle. You now have the strength to lift the bottle easily. In fact, you will probably have enough strength left to lift a full bottle in the normal fashion, just as soon as the suckers have bought you one.

> "Tricky? Not when you're you, and in the mood for a free pint"

EGG BALANCE

The Bet

This proposition actually has two parts to it, the first seemingly unimportant, but actually vital to the success of the second. Take your egg – what do you mean, you haven't brought an egg with you? I've told you before, an egg is the hustler's friend. Go and ask in the kitchen and hope they're properly stocked, then present it to your friends. How clever would it be to be able to balance that egg on the table, standing on its base? It would be pretty clever, agreed. But perhaps not clever enough for a free drink. How about if you could balance it, again on its base, on the rim of a bottle? Not the whole rim of the bottle – any idiot could do that – but actually on one part of the rim.

Why, that would take a genius... You just happen to know one of those, and he's very, very thirsty.

The Solution

First of all, you explain, balancing the egg on the table is actually very easy and – for free, you insist, it's really not worth the price of a drink – you show them how. Get a salt cellar (if the place had a kitchen with an egg in it, it sure as hell has salt) and make a small pile of salt on the table. Lick your thumb and wipe it on the base of the egg to wet it. Then stand the egg in the salt so that it balances upright. Blow the salt away from the base. There, you say, far too easy, and a bit of a cheat really... But that wasn't the bet, the bet was to balance the egg on the rim of a bottle. Take the egg and, making sure everyone stands back so that the table is utterly steady, balance it on the rim of a bottle. The key is the salt that is now stuck to the base of the egg. While it will still take a steady hand, the base of the egg is no longer perfectly curved and it will stand up on the rim.

mirror image

The Bet

You sit directly opposite your wallet... sorry, friend... and challenge them to copy exactly what you do, move for move. They're bound to manage that, aren't they? Kids in the playground can do it, for God's sake...

The Solution

To begin with, it really doesn't matter what you do, as long as you keep taking sips from your drink. Raise your glass, put it down, move it from one side of the table to the other, pat your head, pick your nose... none of it matters, just keep taking a sip of your drink. Finally, on, say, the third sip, don't swallow. Then make a few more moves before spitting the drink back out into your glass. Unless you were playing with someone who can magically spray alcohol from the inside of their mouth – like a magic booze hamster, and how great would that be? – you've won.

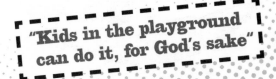

"Kids in the playground can do it, for God's sake"

SPOON FLiP

The Bet

For this bet, you will need a spoon, a fork and a mug. Perhaps it's best performed the morning after your night out when, due to all your free drinks, you're nursing your hangover in a café. Maybe you should make the stake breakfast rather than a round of drinks...

The challenge is to get the spoon into the mug using only the fork. The catch is this: you cannot pick the fork up.

The Solution

Place the spoon next to the mug, the tip of its handle touching the side of the mug. Then place the tip of the fork's handle under the bowl of the spoon, both pieces of cutlery in a straight line leading away from the mug. Now all you have to do is bang down on the tines of the fork so that its handle see-saws up, propelling the spoon into the mug. Don't stab yourself – no hustler looks cool when they're screaming, bleeding and have a fork stuck in their hand.

The Bet

So, do your mates reckon they're quick drinkers? Able to sink a pint in seconds? Time to find out. The challenge: can your victim drink his pint in thirty seconds? If he can, you'll buy him another one.

> "Now would be a good time to duck, in case your bloated victim takes a swing at you"

The Solution

Chances are your thirsty target will neck his drink in next to no time, looking smug (and perhaps somewhat gaseous) by the end of it. At this point, act somewhat surprised, asking him why he was so quick. The challenge was to drink the pint in thirty seconds, a very specific request, which he has failed by doing it in less than thirty seconds. After all, you didn't say he had to do it within the allotted time, did you? That would have been a different challenge entirely. Now would be a good time to duck, in case your bloated victim takes a swing at you.

the Jumping olive

The Bet

Get yourself to a classy bar, the sort that serves olives in a ramekin dish to go alongside your cocktail. (Do this down the Dog and Duck and you've no chance; the trick won't work with a half of mild and a cheese and onion crisp.) Place two beer mats 10 or so centimetres away from one another and then drop an olive in the centre of one of them. You're set, here's the challenge: can the olive be moved from one beer mat to the other? It cannot touch the table, you cannot use your hands and you cannot move the beer mats. Nor can you use a straw (should anyone fancy trying to suck up the olive with one).

The Solution

Use an empty glass, the wider the better (a brandy glass would be perfect). Place it over the olive then begin to rotate the glass quickly so that the olive flies up into it and begins rolling around the inside, the centrifugal force holding it in place. Quickly lift the glass while the olive is spinning and slam it back down on the other mat.

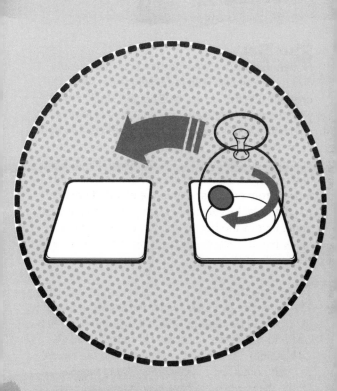

Pints versus shots

The Bet

You're such a fast drinker, I mean, really, the speed with which you can get a pint down you is unbelievable. In fact, you reckon you can drink a pint faster than someone else could drink a shot.

You glance down at your nearly empty beer and – before the unthinkable happens and you run out – you announce that you are willing to place a bet on it. Now, working on the assumption that the entire bar doesn't empty because your reputation has preceded you, you snare your victim. Here's the deal: you'll order three pints and three shots, and whoever drains their drinks first wins (and, naturally, will have to settle the bill). Your victim seems confident – the fool.

Eye them suspiciously and ask if they have some sort of cunning plan up their sleeve. Of course they don't, they just know they can drink three shots quicker than you can drink three pints. Hmm... you're a little suspicious, you say, so we'll make an extra rule: you can't touch each other's glasses. You don't want them trying something funny with your drinks...

OK, they reply... thoroughly convinced you're as mad as an exploding urinal.

The drinks arrive and you win painlessly.

The Solution

As soon as your drinks arrive, finish your nearly empty pint, upturn the glass and, reminding them that they agreed to the rule about not touching each other's glasses, drop it over one of their shots. That's them scuppered, and you sorted for the next three rounds.

A Little Currency Exchange

The Bet

Take a small handful of change out of your pocket and grab any coin that has edges rather than being perfectly round (in the UK, for example, a fifty-pence piece). Now, make a real meal out of trying to balance the coin on the table on its edge. Ask your chosen victim how many they think they could balance in, say, thirty seconds. They can probably manage a few... Okay then, you say, here's the deal: you'll give them double the value of the coin for all the coins they can balance in thirty seconds.

What a deal! Tell them to grab some from the bar, so they have a stack to work with.

Set your timer and go!

"You might even be able to buy a new friend"

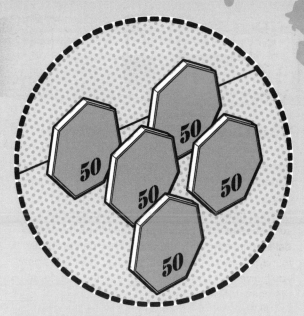

The Solution

However many they manage to stack – and let's hope it's a lot – you hand them a coin or note double the value of the sort of coins they have been balancing (so, in the UK, £1), then scoop all of their coins into your pocket. You have done precisely as you promised, given them double the value of the coin for all the coins they have managed to balance.

With that many, you might even be able to buy a new friend.

The right of Guy Adams to be identified as the Author of the
Work has been asserted by him in accordance with the
Copyright, Designs and Patents Act 1988.

First published in 2010 by HEADLINE PUBLISHING GROUP

1

Publishers Note:
Cataloguing in Publication Data is available from the British Library

ISBN 978 0 7553 6128 1

Design by Nick Venables
Illustrations by Lee Woodgate

Printed and bound in Great Britain by Clays Ltd, St Ives plc

Headline's policy is to use papers that are natural, renewable and
recyclable products and made from wood grown in sustainable forests.
The logging and manufacturing processes are expected to conform to the
environmental regulations of the country of origin.

HEADLINE PUBLISHING GROUP

An Hachette UK Company
338 Euston Road
London NW1 3BH

www.headline.co.uk
www.hachette.co.uk